VIRTUAL HISTORY TOURS

Look around a

SHAKESPEAREAN THEATRE

Stewart Ross

W

FRANKLIN WATTS
LONDON•SYDNEY

First published in 2007 by Franklin Watts

Copyright © 2007 Arcturus Publishing Limited

Franklin Watts
338 Euston Road
London NW1 3BH

Franklin Watts Australia
Level 17/207 Kent Street, Sydney, NSW 2000

Produced by Arcturus Publishing Limited,
26/27 Bickels Yard, 151–153 Bermondsey Street, London SE1 3HA

Series concept: Alex Woolf
Editor: Jenni Rainford
Designer: Ian Winton
Plan artwork: Phil Gleaves

Picture credits:
AKG: 20 (Erich Lessing)
Art Archive: 6 (British Museum / Eileen Tweedy), 7 (Neil Setchfield), 11 (British Museum / Eileen Tweedy),
15 (Garrick Club), 25 (The Art Archive)
Bridgeman Art Library: 12 (Christie's Images), 13 (The Right Honourable Earl of Derby), 17 (Dulwich
Picture Library)
Corbis: 8 (Adam Woolfitt), 10 (Gideon Mendel), 14 (Nik Wheeler), 16 (Robbie Jack), 21 (Dean Conger),
22 (Adam Woolfitt), 24 (Robbie Jack), 26 (Kelley-Mooney Photography), 27 (Robbie Jack), 28 (David Lees),
29 (Bettman)
TopFoto: 18 (TopFoto.co.uk), 19 (Colin Willoughby: ArenaImages / TopFoto.co.uk)
Bailey Publishing Associates: 4, 9, 23

A CIP catalogue record for this book is available from the British Library.

Dewey Decimal Classification Number: 792.09

ISBN 978 0 7496 7197 6

Printed in China

Franklin Watts is a division of Hachette Children's Books.

CONTENTS

THE WOODEN O

Welcome to the ancient city of London. Here, amid gardens and a hotchpotch of little streets and houses, you'll find the famous Globe, one of the city's most popular places of entertainment. Built in 1598, the theatre is where many of William Shakespeare's plays are performed. Shaped like a many-sided letter 'O', it stands about 12.2 metres tall and is hollow in the middle. Look above and you'll see a flag flying from a turret perched high on the roof. At ground level you'll have to jostle with the chattering crowds to pass through the narrow entrances.

New building, old materials

The Globe was the finest playhouse (theatre) of its day. It was built using many of the timbers from the Theatre, a playhouse in north London. The Theatre's landlord did not approve of plays or playhouses, so it was demolished and rebuilt on a new site as the Globe. Finished in 1598, the Globe rested on a frame of huge oak beams. Smaller timbers crossed the spaces between the beams and the gaps were filled with brick, flint, lath (thin slats of wood) and plaster. Beneath the thatched roof the plastered exterior was painted white.

Shakespeare's own handwriting survives only in a few lines of the play *Sir Thomas More*.

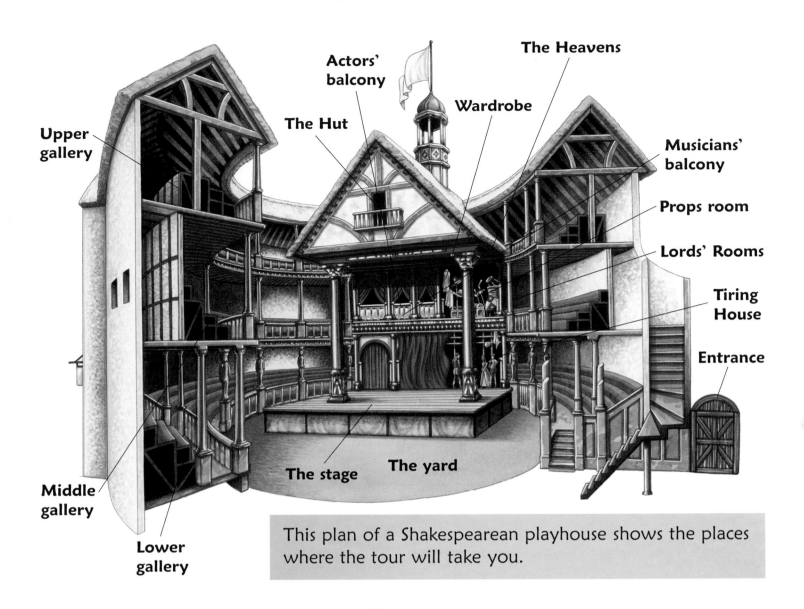

Upper gallery

The Hut

Actors' balcony

The Heavens

Wardrobe

Musicians' balcony

Props room

Lords' Rooms

Tiring House

Entrance

The stage

The yard

Middle gallery

Lower gallery

This plan of a Shakespearean playhouse shows the places where the tour will take you.

The Dutch tourist Johannes de Witt describes the London theatres during a visit to the city.

There are four amphitheatres in London of notable beauty, which from their diverse [different] signs bear different names. In each of them a different play is exhibited to the populace [public]. The two more magnificent of these are situated beyond the Thames, and are called the Rose and the Swan.

Johannes de Witt, 1596.

Latest design

The playhouse's amphitheatre design was based on that of 'baiting houses'. These were places where crowds gathered to watch cruel sports, such as dogs attacking a chained bear. The circular shape, like a mini-stadium, allowed thousands of people to cram into a small space to watch a play. Some sitting, some standing, they came from all walks of life. With so many people in so small a space, the atmosphere inside the packed playhouse was electric.

5

THROUGH THE DOORS

Entrance

You'll enter the playhouse through one of two side entrances for the audience. It's a tight squeeze so that no one can sneak in without paying. This might be a hazard if the building catches fire! You give your entry money to a 'gatherer' stationed by each door. To stand in the noisy, jostling yard you only pay one penny, but for the cheapest seats you pay twopence, and for the most expensive seats it's sixpence.

THE YARD –
SEE PAGE 8

Seats and stairs

The Globe could hold an audience of more than 3,000 people. Most people sat in the galleries that stretched in a circle around the stage. It is believed that, in the Globe, those going to the galleries went up staircases just inside the doors. However, the Swan Theatre had stairs on the outside. There is also evidence that those who sat in the very best seats – in the Lords' Rooms – entered through the actors' Tiring House.

GALLERIES – SEE PAGE 10
LORDS' ROOMS – SEE PAGE 12
TIRING HOUSE – SEE PAGE 22

The 1616 Globe replaced the similar Shakespearean building that had burnt down in 1613.

The modern Globe, opened in 1997, is a close copy of the Shakespearean playhouse theatre.

Sharers

Playhouses were run by companies managed by a group of about 12 'sharers'. The sharers funded the business and shared the profits. A company would build or hire a building, assemble the actors, produce the play and collect the money. If the plays were popular, as Shakespeare's were, then the audiences and profits were large.

Plays for profit

As a sharer in the Lord Chamberlain's Men (later called the King's Men), Shakespeare earned enough money between 1597 and 1605 to buy a property that was worth about £900 in his home town of Stratford-upon-Avon. An average house then cost just £25!

Dr Samuel Johnson, a distinguished 18th-century scholar, recalls a story he had heard about Shakespeare's first job in London.

In the time of Elizabeth ... many came on horseback to the play, and when Shakespeare fled [ran away] to London ... his first expedient [job] was to wait at the door of the play-house, and hold the horses of those that had no servants, that they might be ready again after the performance.

Dr Samuel Johnson, 1765

SHAKESPEARE'S FORTUNE – SEE PAGE 17

THE YARD

Now you find yourself in the 'yard' or the 'pit' of the playhouse. Hold on to your money – there are cutpurses about! The poorest part of the audience, known as 'groundlings', stands here. The groundlings have paid just one penny to enter. The floor is covered with mortar, ash and rubbish. About 700 groundlings can squash into this space. There are no toilet facilities and only the very richest people take baths, so no wonder the groundlings are also known as 'stinkards'!

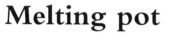

The yard

Melting pot

The playhouse was an extraordinary meeting place for all sections of Elizabethan society. In the yard were the men and women from the labouring classes. The wealthy, and sometimes nobility, occupied the expensive gallery seats that loomed above the groundlings on three sides.

GALLERIES – SEE PAGE 10

This modern cutaway model of a Shakespearean playhouse shows the yard, where the poorest members of the audience stood to watch the play.

Popular entertainment

The daily wage for a labourer was one shilling (12 pennies), so all but the poverty-stricken could afford the one penny needed to enter the yard. Here mingled apprentices, carpenters, brewers, fishwives, nut-sellers, pickpockets, goodtime girls, beer-sellers, cooks and servants. They grew rowdy if they did not enjoy the performance. As a result, Shakespeare's plays included characters like the greasy con man, Sir John Falstaff in *Henry IV* (*Parts I and II*) and *The Merry Wives of Windsor*, and the drunken porter in *Macbeth*, who appealed directly to the groundlings.

Beware cutpurse! In the days before pockets, a fat purse was a tempting target for a villain.

Anthony Munday, a bad actor who was hissed off the stage, attacks theatre audiences.

Whoever shall visit the chapel of Satan, I mean the Theatre, shall find there no want of [lots of] young ruffians, nor lack of harlots [saucy girls], utterly past all shame: who pressed to the front of the scaffolds [stage], to the end to [in order to] show their impudence [cheeky attractiveness], and to be ... an object to all men's eyes.

Anthony Munday in *A Second and Third Blast of Retrait from Plaies and Theaters*, 1580.

Danger zone

London's governors were not keen on playhouses. Plays drew people from their work, and there were fears of rioting among the crowds. Disease also spread quickly within a tightly packed audience. As a result, theatres were closed whenever there was an outbreak of plague in the city.

THE GALLERIES

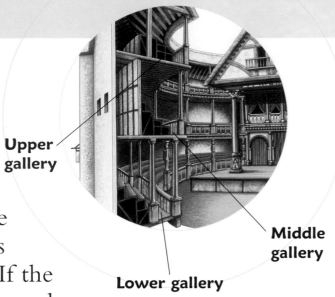

Upper gallery

Middle gallery

Lower gallery

Look up and you'll see the galleries rising to the roof. The majority of the audience sit here on benches. There are three galleries – lower, middle and upper – reached by wooden stairs at the back. From up here the view of the stage is excellent (unless you're sitting behind a wooden pillar!). If the actors speak clearly, you can hear every word. Unlike the groundlings, you are sheltered from the weather by the thatched roof. The atmosphere is more refined, too, with polite conversation and a whiff of perfume in the air.

Seats for the wealthy

The two lower galleries each held some 800 people, and the upper about 500. As a seat in the galleries cost at least twopence, they were occupied by wealthier citizens – merchants, bankers, gentlemen with property, courtiers and their women. However, having money to spend on fine clothes and jewels was unusual because most of the population at the time lived close to poverty.

The gallery audience in the modern Globe sit on Elizabethan-style hard wooden benches.

See and be seen

Those with money liked to show off their wealth. It is likely that they took cushioned seats at the front of a gallery near the stage, where they could be seen by the rest of the audience. Foreign travellers visiting London were surprised to see wealthy women sitting in a gallery attended only by a pageboy. In most parts of Europe, smart women always had at least one manservant in attendance to look after them.

WOMEN – SEE PAGE 22

Thomas Platter, a visitor from Basle, Switzerland, carefully recorded all he saw in London.

There are different galleries and places, however, where the seating is better and more comfortable and therefore more expensive. For whoever cares to stand below only pays one English penny, but if he wishes to sit he enters by another door, and pays another penny.... And during the performance food and drink are carried round the audience ...

Thomas Platter at the Curtain Theatre, 1599.

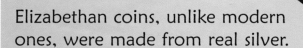

Elizabethan coins, unlike modern ones, were made from real silver.

Hall theatres

During the 17th century, Shakespeare's company managed two theatres. As well as the Globe, which was an amphitheatre, they also staged plays in Blackfriars, which was known as a hall theatre. This was an enclosed building that held around 750 people. Hall theatres were better for staging plays in the winter months, although the candle lights made the atmosphere heavy and smoky. Prices ranged from sixpence to half-a-crown (30 pennies), making them popular only with the extremely wealthy.

THE LORDS' ROOMS

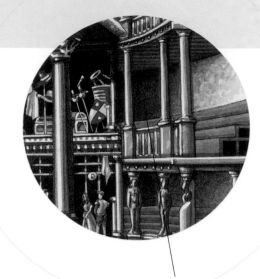

Lords' Rooms

As you stand at the front of the stage and look back towards the Tiring House, you'll see a long gallery above the entrance doors. This gallery is divided into rooms, like the boxes in a modern theatre. These are the Lords' Rooms and are the most expensive seats in the entire playhouse. It costs sixpence to sit here and each room has comfortable chairs that face the audience. You probably enter the Lords' Rooms through a back entrance via the Tiring House, which is normally used only by the cast and stagehands.

TIRING HOUSE – SEE PAGE 22

Gentlemen

Beside the Lords' Rooms were the slightly cheaper Gentlemen's Rooms. Like 'lord', in Elizabethan times, 'gentleman' was an official title. Gentlemen, for instance, were allowed to have their own coats of arms. In 1598 William Shakespeare paid for his father, John, to acquire a coat of arms. This allowed father and son to call themselves 'gentlemen'.

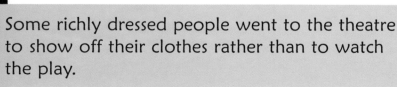

Some richly dressed people went to the theatre to show off their clothes rather than to watch the play.

Attention please!

Reports suggest that those in the Lords' Rooms did not always pay much attention to the play anyway, even though they could hear every word. They often chatted, ate and drank, and played card games such as *primero*, which was similar to modern-day poker!

Playing *primero* was a popular pastime in the Lords' Rooms.

Orazio Busino, the chaplain to the Venetian embassy in London, describes a visit to the Fortune Theatre:

[I was impressed in the theatre] ... to see such a crowd of nobility, so very well arrayed [dressed] that they looked like so many princes, listening as silently and as soberly as possible. These theatres are frequented [visited] by a number of respectable and handsome ladies, who come freely and seat themselves among the men without the slightest hesitation.

Busino, a visitor from Venice, at the Fortune Theatre, c.1617

Who's here?

Although they were behind the actors most of the time, those in the Lords' Rooms could hear the play better than the rest of the audience. However, the view from the Lords' Rooms was not always good. Some scholars suggest this is why characters explain what is going on during the play. As an actor enters, for example, someone already on stage often says, 'Who's here?' This allows the new entrant to say their name, in case some of the audience cannot see their face. If they did not do this, those in the Lords' Rooms might ask out loud what was going on!

13

THE STAGE

The first thing you'll notice about the stage is its enormous size: about 12.2 metres wide by 9.1 metres deep. Since the yard is about 21.3 metres across, the stage takes up almost half of it and is 1.5 metres high. From near the front, on either side rise two huge pillars, each made from a single giant oak tree. You can see that these support a vast painted canopy made from canvas, which covers the entire stage, protecting it from the sun and rain.

The stage

Down to hell

The stage stood on wooden supports that were hidden by boards or a heavy curtain. The space beneath the stage was used for storage or as a source of music or live sound effects. The understage space might also be accessed from a trapdoor in the centre of the acting platform. This opening, known as 'hell', had many uses. It could be a hole (the grave in Shakespeare's *Hamlet*, for example) or an opening into which things (like the witches' cauldron in Shakespeare's *Macbeth*) or people might disappear.

The stage of the modern Globe Theatre, like the original, has two huge wooden pillars.

Making an entrance

Actors normally entered the stage from two or three doors in the Tiring House, which was just behind it. Actors might also be 'discovered', like Hermione in Shakespeare's *The Winter's Tale*. She was hidden behind curtains that were hung in front of the Tiring House doors.

TIRING HOUSE – SEE PAGE 22

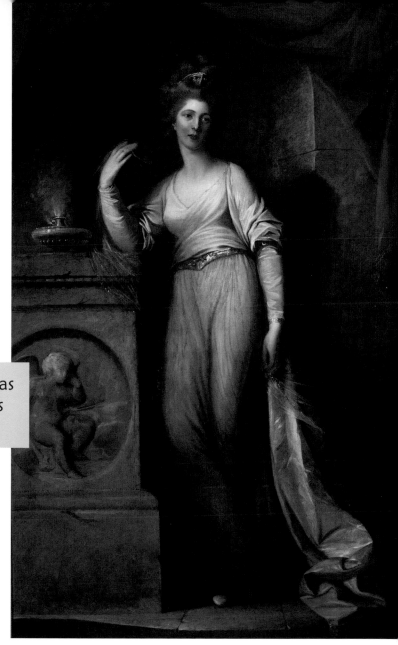

In *The Winter's Tale* Hermione was 'revealed' by opening the curtains at the back of the stage.

If the unknown author of *The Cyprian Conqueror* is to be believed, 17th-century acting was less realistic than today.

The other parts of action [your skill] is in the gesture[s], which must be various, as required.... In a sorrowful part, your head must hang down; in a proud [part], your head must be lofty; in an amorous [part], closed eyes, hanging down looks and crossed arms ...

The anonymous author of
The Cyprian Conqueror, c.1633

Face to face

Moving downstage (getting nearer to the audience), an Elizabethan actor could bend down and touch the groundlings. There was no gap separating the actors from the audience and no artificial lighting to add special effects or help them to be seen. Both the actors and the audience were face to face in a theatrical experience that was both thrilling and immediate.

ACTORS' BALCONY

As you step onto the balcony at the back of the stage, you'll have a great view of the play. But in some plays the action itself takes place on the balcony. Perhaps the most famous 'balcony scene' is in Shakespeare's *Romeo and Juliet*, where Juliet appears 'at a window'. Looking up, Romeo says that the window is the east and Juliet is the rising sun.

Actors' balcony

Just an illusion

The balcony was a useful way for actors to make the audience believe in the set. In Shakespeare's *Richard II* the king appeared 'on the walls' of Flint Castle before making another entrance 'below'. To do this, the actor first entered onto the balcony then went back inside, tip-toed quietly down the wooden stairs in the Tiring House, and reappeared through one of the normal entrances.

'O Romeo, Romeo! wherefore art thou Romeo?' In the original production, Juliet was on the balcony at the back of the stage.

16

Rubbing shoulders

When actors were performing on the balcony, they may have mixed with the occupants of the Lords' Rooms. Some suggest that, when a play required it, part of the balcony was left free for the actors. When this happened, the company took less money! Whoever was allowed up there, the balcony was not used for major action. Balcony scenes were fairly short and involved little or no movement from the actor aloft.

LORDS' ROOMS – SEE PAGE 12

This portrait shows Nathan Field, a star actor of the early 17th century, who was famous for having many girlfriends.

In a popular pamphlet, the well-known highwayman Gamaliel Ratsey says actors are in the same social class as himself:

Some of you [actors are] not content to do well, but [always] striving to over-do and go beyond yourselves.... Yet ... others ... I must needs confess are very well deserving both for true action and fair delivery of speech. And yet I warrant [believe] ... the very best [of you] have sometimes been content to go home at night with [just] fifteen pence.

Attributed to the highwayman Gamaliel Ratsey, 1605

Honest workers

Aloft or below, the life of an actor was not easy. Strict Protestants, known as Puritans, condemned them as liars because their job was all about pretending to be someone they were not. Educated men and women, especially at the king or queen's court, respected the actors' art but did not believe they belonged very high up the social scale. However, to a few, including Shakespeare (who began his theatre career as an actor), the stage brought fame, fortune and status.

PURITANS – SEE PAGE 29

MUSICIANS' BALCONY

The balcony above the stage is a crowded place. Beside the smart set in the Lords' Rooms and the actors aloft, you'll see a band of musicians seated up here ready to play whenever needed. Music is an essential part of Elizabethan theatre and most plays written at this time require music of some sort. There are trumpet calls, dances, interludes, mood music and songs. The beat is usually quite strong and the sound is a bit squeaky compared with modern music.

Musicians' balcony

Song and dance

Musicians were better paid than actors. If a company had its own musicians, or hired them for a show, it needed to make the best use of them. By the 17th century there was often music before a show, between acts and for a dance at the end. Singing on stage to a musical accompaniment was difficult because, facing the audience, the singer could not see the musicians. However, if he turned towards them to make sure he was in time, most of the audience could not hear his song!

A pipe and drum accompanied the 16th-century comic actor William Kemp as he danced along the road.

18

The consort

Music during the show was sometimes performed by a consort (group) who played some of the following instruments: hautboys or shawms (both like oboes), recorders, cornetts (like woodwind trumpets), sackbuts (like trombones), viols (early types of violin) and bandores or citterns (both like lutes). Trumpets and drums announced the arrival of important characters in a play. Some actors accompanied their own songs on the lute or cittern.

Elizabethan dancing is still performed today on the stage at London's Globe Theatre.

The long Elizabethan poem *The Passionate Pilgrim*, which Shakespeare may have helped to write, describes the beauty of music:

If music and sweet poetry agree,
As they must needs, the sister and the brother,
Then must the love be great 'twixt [between] thee and me,
Because thou lovest the one, and I the other.

William Shakespeare,
The Passionate Pilgrim,
printed 1599

The masque

As indoor hall theatres became more popular, a new type of drama – the masque – arrived from continental Europe. This was a sophisticated entertainment that mixed drama, dance, music and art. It influenced popular theatre, too. Shakespeare's last complete play, *The Tempest*, is full of surprise, pageant and, above all, music. It is set on an island that Caliban (one of the play's characters) says, '… is full of noises, / Sounds and sweet airs that give delight and hurt not.'

HALL THEATRES – SEE PAGE 11

THE HUT

The Hut

High up, above the canopy over the stage, far from the hubbub below, stands a small thatched cabin. This is the Hut, the tallest part of the playhouse. It is full of strange-looking machinery and other theatre apparatus. Standing up here, perhaps on a platform by the door, a trumpeter's proud blast announces that the play is about to begin. Above him flutters a black flag. Its colour is significant – today's play is a tragedy.

To your seats! A trumpeter announces the start of a play.

Sound effects

In the centre of the Hut floor was the winding gear for lowering and raising props, scenery, and even people, to and from the stage below. Nearby were the devices for making sound effects. The noise of thunder was made by shaking a thin sheet of metal or rolling a cannon ball down a wooden gully. There was also a cannon, which, although not loaded with shot, could still be dangerous. When the cannon was fired during a performance of Shakespeare's *Henry VIII* in 1613, sparks flew onto the Globe's thatched roof – and the famous playhouse burnt to the ground!

20

MUSIC – SEE PAGE 18

Comedy, tragedy, history

The flags flown from the playhouse mast were more than decoration. Perhaps 50 per cent of the Globe's audience were illiterate, unable to read and write. The flag was a means of telling these people what type of play was on: black for tragedy (serious), white for comedy (more light-hearted but not necessarily funny all the way through) and red for history (based on real events).

In the footsteps of the master – the schoolroom in which Shakespeare may have been taught at Stratford Grammar School.

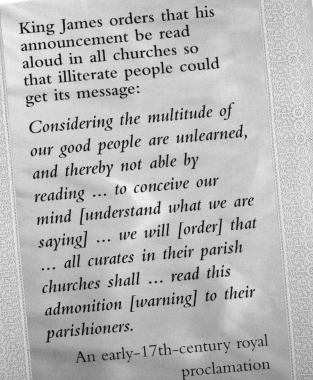

King James orders that his announcement be read aloud in all churches so that illiterate people could get its message:

Considering the multitude of our good people are unlearned, and thereby not able by reading ... to conceive our mind [understand what we are saying] ... we will [order] that ... all curates in their parish churches shall ... read this admonition [warning] to their parishioners.

An early-17th-century royal proclamation

Elizabethan censorship

Shakespeare's later plays do not really fit into any of the three categories. Whatever its type, before a new play could be performed, it had to be approved by the Master of the Revels. At a difficult time in Elizabeth I's reign, Shakespeare's *Richard II* was banned because it showed rebels removing a king from the throne.

TIRING HOUSE

Tiring House

Go through one of the openings at the back of the stage and you find yourself in the Tiring House. This narrow space is divided into two or more rooms. There are further rooms above, accessed by a staircase from the ground floor. During a performance this whole area bustles with activity. Actors enter and exit the stage, adjust or change their dress, or sit quietly in a corner running through their lines. Around them, stagehands hurry about with props and pieces of scenery.

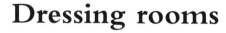

PROPS – SEE PAGE 24

Dressing rooms

The Tiring House gets its name from 'attire', which means both 'clothes' and 'to get dressed'. The Tiring House was where actors changed into their costumes for a performance. They could all share the same space because, before 1660, there were no women actors on the English stage. Women's roles were played by boys.

Stagehands at work setting the stage in the modern Globe Theatre.

The play's the thing

The actors had little time off. They rehearsed in the morning and put on a different play each afternoon. Actors were given only their own lines rather than the complete text. This was to stop other companies from stealing the play and performing it themselves. Plays changed from performance to performance, too. Because of this, it is often difficult to work out exactly what words Shakespeare actually wrote.

Shakespeare loved comparing the stage to the wider world – and vice versa:

All the world's a stage,

And all the men and women merely players;

They have their exits and their entrances,

And one man in his time plays many parts,

His acts being seven ages.

Jaques in Shakespeare's
As You Like It

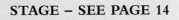
STAGE – SEE PAGE 14

A close community

A company putting on a play was a very close-knit community. The members of the King's Men, Shakespeare's company, all knew one another well because they spent so much time together. When the theatres were closed for the winter, the company travelled widely across a broad area of southern England. From Ipswich to Oxford, Shrewsbury to Barnstaple they performed in inns, halls and stately homes.

KING'S MEN – SEE PAGE 7

An Elizabethan boy actor puts on a dress in order to play a woman's role.

PROPS ROOM

On the first floor of the Tiring House, behind the entrance to the balcony, you'll discover a room stuffed with an extraordinary collection of fascinating objects. These are the 'properties' – normally shortened to 'props' – required for this season's plays: all the items needed by the actors on stage. You'll see a vast range of props, from shields and wooden rainbows to cauldrons and bearskins!

Props room

Making it seem real

To produce a memorable performance, if a character went to hell, for example, a huge Hell's Mouth was hauled onto the stage for them to disappear down. Sword fights had to look skilful, exciting and genuine – the bursting of a hidden, blood-filled pig's bladder guaranteed that on-stage stabbings were suitably gruesome! And when a character made his exit 'pursued by a bear', he had to be chased off by another actor in a bearskin.

Hamlet, played by Mark Rylance, with the skull of Yorick. Skulls were just one of many props a theatre company needed.

Spectacle

We have enormous admiration for the wonderful words of Shakespeare's plays. It is easy to forget that many of his contemporaries were just as interested in what they saw as what they heard. The Elizabethans loved pageant and show, and the theatre was one of the few places where they could find such spectacle regularly. Theatre companies met this need by making their performances visually memorable.

The cauldron is an important prop in Shakespeare's *Macbeth*. It often disappeared through the trapdoor in the stage floor. This 18th-century illustration shows Macbeth re-visiting the witches in order to learn his fate.

Philip Henslowe of the Lord Chamberlain's Men makes a list of all the company's props.

Item, 1 rock, 1 cage, 1 tomb, 1 Hell mouth

Item, 1 tomb of Guido, 1 tomb of Dido, 1 bedstead …

Item, 1 golden fleece, 2 rackets, 1 bay tree …

Item, 1 Neptune fork & garland …

Item, Cupid's bow & quiver; cloth of the Sun and Moon …

Item, 1 lion … 1 great horse with his legs ..

Item, 1 ghost's crown …

From theatre manager Philip Henslowe's list of props, 1598

Imagination

However realistic the props were, a play was simply an illusion. In some plays, such as Shakespeare's *Henry V*, an introduction reminds the audience that what they are about to see needs their imagination to make it work: 'Think, when we talk of horses, that you see them.' In the end, a Shakespeare play's success depended very heavily on the players' ability to act.

THE WARDROBE

The wardrobe

Beside the Props room is a locked door. Behind it lie the company's most valuable possessions — its costumes. Inside the wardrobe, your eyes sweep over a wonderful array of dresses, robes, cloaks, jerkins, doublets, togas, shoes, boots, hose and hats. In front of you is the gorgeous scarlet dress worn by the boy who plays Lady Macbeth. Opposite the dress is a breastplate worn by Richard III at the Battle of Bosworth (in Shakespeare's *Richard III*) and King Henry V at the Battle of Agincourt (in Shakespeare's *Henry V*).

Status symbols

Elizabethan law stated that everyone had to dress according to their class. It was illegal for a merchant, for example, to dress like a lord, or a servant like a master. This idea was reflected in the theatre, where the type, colour and quality of a person's costume reflected their social status. Theatre companies even had to be licensed so that actors could wear costumes above their class.

Costumes were the most valuable possessions of a Shakespearean theatre company. Today, Shakespearean costumes are carefully recreated by expert costume makers.

Looking the part

Company manager Philip Henslowe spent more on costumes than on play scripts. This is not surprising when a cloak embroidered with silver and gold cost him an amazing £20.50 – almost as much as a house! Shakespearean characters did not dress realistically for the stage. Instead, they had to be immediately recognizable as a type. A king from any period in history, for instance, had to be instantly seen as a king by his magnificent clothes. Similarly, a servant had to dress like an Elizabethan servant.

DRESSING ROOM – SEE PAGE 22

Manager Henslowe makes a careful inventory of his company's most valuable possessions.

Cloaks
1 A scarlet cloak with 2 broad gold laces: with gold buttons of the same down the sides ...
Gowns...
3 A crimson robe striped with gold, faced with ermine ...
Antique suits ...
1 A coat of crimson velvet cut in panes and embroidered in gold.

From theatre manager Philip Henslowe's list of costumes, 1598

Colourful costumes

Colour sent out important signals to the audience: black signified death or wickedness, red was blood (worn by murderers), white was purity (worn by young girls) and yellow was the sun, a colour associated with lovers. So because of the colours that were worn by different characters on stage, the audience could tell precisely what sort of person they were, even before the player had spoken.

The crimson dress, worn by Frances Barber as Cleopatra in 2006, may have suggested royalty and, perhaps, danger.

27

UP IN THE HEAVENS

The Heavens

Looking up from the stage, you see the 'Heavens' spread out above you. Groundlings and the audience in the lower galleries, and on the balcony, glimpse the same scene, too. It's the underside of the huge canopy hanging over the stage, painted in vibrant colours with a variety of images like the sun and moon. As the stage represents the world ('the globe') and the trapdoor in it represents the entrance to hell, the canopy represents the sky and, above it, heaven.

STAGE – SEE PAGE 14

Machinery above

The Heavens also served a practical purpose. It was a false ceiling, hiding storage space for theatre materials. There was a trapdoor in the middle through which objects and actors could be lowered onto the stage, with startling effect.

At the end of Shakespeare's *As You Like It*, written in about 1600, Hymen, the god of marriage, appears suddenly. During its first production at the Globe, Hymen would probably have descended from the Heavens, gently lowered in some sort of sling to the accompaniment of mystical music.

The Greek god Atlas carrying the globe on his shoulders. This image is captured in the name of the most famous Shakespearean theatre.

The Renaissance

The pictures on the Heavens, the marble-painted pillars that supported the canopy, and the image of the globe itself (Atlas carrying the world on his shoulders) all reflected the latest movement in European learning. This was known as the Renaissance – a new interest in the Classical World of ancient Greece and Rome. The Renaissance began in Italy and spread slowly north.

Puritans such as Oliver Cromwell believed that theatres were sinful and he ordered their closure in 1642.

The London lawyer John Manningham records in his diary the plays he has seen.

At our feast we had a play called 'Twelve Night, or What You Will'. [It was] much like The Comedy of Errors ... in Plautus [a Roman author], but most like and near to that in Italian called Ingannati.

John Manningham, Diary, 1602–03

Classical plays

Elizabethan plays are full of classical references. Some of Shakespeare's dramas, like *The Comedy of Errors*, are based on classical plays. This gave the Puritans even more reason to dislike the theatre. The Classical Period was pre-Christian and, in the Puritans' eyes, its arts encouraged sinful luxury and extravagance. The Puritans took over the government of London in 1642, and closed all theatres. They remained shut for 18 years.

PURITANS – SEE PAGE 17

TIMELINE

1558	Elizabeth I becomes queen.
1564	William Shakespeare is born.
1577	The Curtain amphitheatre playhouse opens in north London.
1587	The Rose amphitheatre playhouse opens on the south bank of the River Thames.
1588	Attempted invasion of England by Spanish Armada fails.
1590	Shakespeare, now in London, begins writing *Henry IV.*
1592	Shakespeare writes *Richard III.*
1593–4	London theatres closed because of outbreak of plague.
1594	The Lord Chamberlain's Men (theatre company) formed. Shakespeare writes *Romeo and Juliet.*
1595	The Swan amphitheatre playhouse opens on the south bank of the River Thames. Shakespeare writes *Richard II.*
1596	John Shakespeare granted the right to bear a coat of arms, officially making him and his son William 'gentlemen'.
1597	Shakespeare writes *Henry IV (Part I).*
1598	The Globe amphitheatre playhouse opens on the south bank of the River Thames.
1599	Shakespeare writes *As You like It.*
1600	Shakespeare writes *Hamlet.*
1603	King James I succeeds Elizabeth I. The Lord Chamberlain's Men become the King's Men.
1605	Shakespeare writes *Macbeth.*
1607	Jamestown, oldest English settlement in America, founded.
1608	The King's Men buy Blackfriars, a hall theatre.
1610	Shakespeare writes *The Winter's Tale.*
1611	Shakespeare's *The Tempest* performed at court.
1613	Globe Theatre burnt down, rebuilt in 1616.
1616	William Shakespeare dies.
1623	Shakespeare's collected plays published in the First Folio.
1642	London's theatres closed due to the Puritans' Act of Parliament (until 1660).

GLOSSARY

amphitheatre Theatre with the raised audience circling the stage.

attire Clothing.

Classical plays Plays from or in the style of ancient Greece and Rome.

coat of arms An elaborate badge showing a person's social position.

comedy A play that ends with most characters pleased, and good triumphing over evil.

company A group, including actors and managers, that puts on plays.

consort A musical band.

cutpurse A pickpocket.

doublet A tight jacket.

Elizabethan From the reign of Queen Elizabeth I (1558-1603).

gallery The balcony.

gatherers Those who collected the entrance money at the doors of Shakespearean theatres.

groundlings Members of the audience without seats. They stood around the stage, and were also known as 'stinkards'.

hall theatre Hall-shaped enclosed theatre with the stage at one end.

Heavens Painted canopy above the stage.

history A play that was based on real historical events.

hose Woolly tights, often worn by actors.

jerkin Tight, sleeveless jacket.

King's Men The theatre company that was looked after by King James I (1603-1625).

lath and plaster Type of wall made by applying plaster over a network of thin strips of wood (laths) woven together.

Lords' Rooms Best seats in the gallery, behind the stage.

masque Stage pageant (costumed procession).

Master of the Revels Person responsible for entertainments provided at the royal court.

pageant Colourful and lively procession or show, normally with music.

plague Disease known as the Bubonic Plague (also as the Black Death) that swept across Europe from time to time between the 14th and 19th centuries.

players Actors.

playhouse A theatre.

props Properties or objects needed by actors on stage.

Puritan Strict Protestant Christian who wanted to 'purify' the church and the way people behaved.

Renaissance New interest in ancient Greece and Rome.

sharers Those who invested money in a theatre company and shared its profits.

stagehand Person helping arrange the stage before or during a performance.

Tiring House Rooms at the back of the stage for dressing and other purposes.

toga Robe worn by men in ancient Rome.

tragedy A play about the fall of a great person, usually through a single, glaring fault of their own.

yard The space around the stage where the poorest members of the audience stood to watch a play.

FURTHER INFORMATION

Books

Shakespeare by Peter Chrisp (Dorling Kindersley, 2004)

William Shakespeare by Emma Fischel (Watts, 2002)

Shakespeare's Globe by Toby Forward (Walker, 2005)

Shakespeare's Theatre by Andrew Langley (Oxford University Press, 1999)

William Shakespeare by Stewart Ross (Evans, 1998)

Shakespeare's England by Stewart Ross (Heinemann, 2004)

William Shakespeare by Stewart Ross (Hodder, 2004)

Shakespeare and Macbeth by Stewart Ross (Chrysalis, 1998)

Elizabethan England: A History of the Elizabethan Theater by Adam Woog (Lucent, 2002)

Websites

http://shakespeare.palomar.edu/theatre.htm
http://www.onlineshakespeare.com
http://www.william-shakespeare.info/site-map.htm
http://www.shakespeares-globe.org

Some places to visit

Shakespearean-style theatres have been built in London, Toronto, San Diego (California), Odessa (Texas), Rome and in many other cities around the world.

At Stratford-Upon-Avon, Warwickshire, England, there are several sites associated with William Shakespeare.

INDEX